THE FAITH WE HOLD

ARCHBISHOP PAUL
OF
FINLAND

THE FAITH WE HOLD

Translated from the Finnish
by
Marita Nykänen and Esther Williams

With a Foreword
by
Fr. Alexander Schmemann

ST. VLADIMIR'S SEMINARY PRESS
CRESTWOOD, N. Y.
1980

This book was first published in Finland, in 1978, under the title
MITEN USKOMME.

Library of Congress Cataloging in Publication Data

Paavali, Abp. of Karelia and All Finland, 1914-1988
    The faith we hold.

Translation of Miten uskomme.
    1. Orthodox Eastern Church—Doctrinal and contro-
versial works. 2. Spiritual life—Orthodox Eastern
authors. I. Title.
BX320.2.P3313   230'.19   80-10404
ISBN 0-913836-63-X

ISBN 0-913836-63-X

First Printing   1980
Second Printing 1981
Third Printing   1989

PRINTED IN THE UNITED STATES OF AMERICA
BY
ATHENS PRINTING COMPANY
NEW YORK, NY

CONTENTS

III PRAYER

FOREWORD TO THE ENGLISH EDITION

Let your light so shine before men, that they may see your good works, and glorify your Father which is in heaven. (Mt 5:16)

The author of this book, Archbishop Paul, has been since 1960 the Primate of the Orthodox Church of Finland. By comparison with the other Orthodox Churches the Finnish Church is small — some 70,000 communicants scattered all over Finland and living in the midst of an overwhelming Lutheran majority. At a time, however, when almost everywhere in the world, in the traditionally Orthodox lands as well as in its Western "diaspora," the Orthodox Church is undergoing a deep crisis, the small Finnish Church appears to be a haven, not only of order and stability, but above all of spiritual vitality and inner growth. And for this it is indebted in no small measure to its "Father Archbishop," as his flock affectionately call him, to his truly unique spiritual and pastoral leadership.

A Karelian Orthodox by birth, Archbishop Paul early in life took monastic vows at Valamo, the old and famous monastery on Lake Ladoga, which for several centuries was the spiritual center of Northwestern Russia and Karelia, the Orthodox province of Finland. And, as he himself acknowledges, he would probably have stayed there for his entire life, had not the fateful "Northern War" of 1939 between Finland and the USSR forced the evacuation of the Valamo monastic community to Finland's mainland and involved it almost against its will in the life of the Finnish Church. Thus it is a monk—by vocation, by "heart's desire"—a monk spiritually shaped by the most authentic monastic spirit and tradition, that in 1960 was elected second Archbishop of Karelia and all Finland. At that time the Church of Finland was still recovering not only from the crisis inflicted upon her by the war (the evacuation of virtually the entire Karelian population from its "organic" Orthodox home in Eastern Karelia) but also from difficulties which it encountered since the proclamation in 1918 of its independence from the Russian Church. What the Church had to face was a double "non-recognition": psychological and cultural non-recognition on the part of the Finnish Lutheran majority which perceived Orthodoxy as a "Russian," i.e. foreign, religion, and also canonical non-recognition by the Russian Church which until 1958 protested against the autonomy granted to its former diocese by the Patriarchate of Constantinople.

It was therefore a task of *reconstruction* — national, spiritual, canonical — that the new Archbishop had to face and to perform. And now, twenty years later, one can say without any exaggeration that in fulfilling this task he succeeded beyond all human expectations. In spite of its numerical weakness the Orthodox Church of Finland is today an organic part of the national fabric, as truly Finnish as it is truly Orthodox. It consists of three dioceses and has a well organized administrative center in Kuopio, the see of the Primate. Its theological seminary, which in September of 1978 celebrated its fiftieth anniversary, is remarkably free from any kind of provincialism, open to and creatively aware of all positive developments in contemporary Orthodox theology. The monastery of New Valamo and the convent at Lintuli attract thousands of pilgrims every year. At the same time a profound and genuine revival is taking place in the areas of liturgy, liturgical music, and iconography. And the architect as well as the inspiring bearer of this Finnish Orthodox identity, of this creative and living synthesis integrating the various "heritages" preserved by the Finnish Church, is unmistakably Archbishop Paul. Not only is he a nationally respected religious leader in Finland itself, but his voice is also heard more and more, and with growing respect and attention, by the entire Orthodox Church.

This success, however, is due not only to Archbishop Paul's administrative abilities, but above all to his spiritual vision combined, in what seems today a unique manner, with his pastoral charism. Not a theologian, not a canonist, not a liturgist in the narrow, "academic" sense of these terms, he is nevertheless all of that on a much deeper, much more authentic level: on the level of a fully accepted— as obedience, as total responsibility — *episcopal ministry*. For it is not some particular interest in any of these "disciplines" but rather his total identification with the Church, with what is *good* for her and for the human souls entrusted to him, that makes him into a theologian, a canonist, a liturgist, and that marks all his words with that courage, simplicity, directness and — I would add — "self-evidence," which are so obviously lacking in so many of today's Orthodox discussions and debates.

All these charisms are richly evidenced in this little book. Seldom have I seen so many absolutely essential *truths* not merely defined but truly *revealed* on so few pages and with such simplicity and directness. Reading this book, one is astonished that so many of these *truths* still remain objects of controversies and disagreements. The purpose of this foreword is only to "make felt," be it only a little, the gracious personality of the man who wrote these pages. God has given me the privilege and the joy of knowing him personally, of witnessing his ministry as Priest, Teacher and Pastor to his Church. Through this book, however, this ministry is extended to the whole Orthodox Church, so that we all, having read it, can join his flock in calling him "Father Archbishop."

Fr. Alexander Schmemann, Dean
St. Vladimir's
Orthodox Theological Seminary

Christmas, 1979

INTRODUCTION

The aim of *The Faith We Hold* is to describe Orthodoxy from the inside to those outside, and to offer answers to the most fundamental questions. At the same time there will be things of current importance to say to the Orthodox themselves, especially about matters in which our practices need to return to a deeper interpretation of the faith. In this respect this publication may also be called an episcopal pastoral letter.

Christ left no written statement of His teaching, nor did the apostles set about drawing up a creed at first. Instead, as soon as they received power at the outpouring of the Holy Spirit, they began to bear witness to Christ, to His death and resurrection. Those who believed the testimony of the apostles were baptized and received the Holy Spirit. (Acts 1:8; 2:38, 41)

Through the testimony of the apostles new communities and congregations arose everywhere, and thus the Church got its start. In the New Testament the Church is called *ecclesia*, a Greek word originally meaning an assembly of people. The word "church," on the other hand, means "belonging to the Lord." Thus the original distinguishing feature of the Church, implied in its very name, is that of assembling in one place as the Lord's own people.

Wherever the first Christians met, there was the Church or the assembly of the people of God. In this coming together the Christians encountered the Christ in whom they believed. They experienced this encounter in a special way in the Eucharist, which they celebrated with "the breaking of bread" and with "glad and generous hearts." (Acts 2:42, 46) Thus it was a joyous service of thanksgiving — this is the meaning of the Greek word *eucharistia* —

and it was always celebrated under the leadership of the local bishop.

Not even in our day is the Christian faith a philosophy or an ideology; it is an encounter with Christ. The same three things — faith, *ecclesia* and *eucharistia* — still lead to this encounter. Together they are a framework instituted by God, through which the new life of Christ is given to the world.

The new life is founded on acts of God and on divine revelation received with faith. The Biblical conceptions of faith thus form the starting-point of Orthodox Christianity; and so the first part of this book is entitled "faith." *Ecclesia* and *eucharistia*, Church and Communion, are closely connected with each other, because the Church fulfils itself by being a eucharistic community. Hence the title of the second part of the book is "the eucharist." Important as the experience of community in the Church and through the Eucharist is, we must remember the part played by each Christian in maintaining the spiritual life. The third part of the book deals with this matter and is entitled "prayer." However, each part in fact concerns the same total life of the Christian.

Since even the best description of life is only a reflection of the experience itself, the best advice to anyone wishing to get acquainted with Orthodoxy would be the same as that given by Philip to Nathaniel: "Come and see!" (Jn 1:46) Knowing the inadequacy of descriptions, we have all the more reason to pray to the Spirit of truth *to enlighten the eyes of our hearts, that we may know what is the hope to which He has called us, what are the riches of His glorious inheritance in the saints and what is the immeasurable greatness of His power in us who believe.* Cf. Eph 1:17-19

I Faith

Always be prepared to make a defence to any one who calls you to account for the hope that is in you, yet do it with gentleness and reverence.

1 PET 3:15

THE CHURCH

The Orthodox Church simply calls itself "the Church," just as the Greeks in the past used the word "Christians" to refer to the Orthodox. This follows naturally from the fact that the Eastern Orthodox Church is organically the same congregation or *ecclesia* which was born at the outpouring of the Holy Spirit in Jerusalem on Pentecost. In many places already mentioned in the New Testament this congregation has remained the same throughout history. The Orthodox Church does not need to give proof of its historical authenticity; it is simply the direct continuation of the Church of the Apostolic Age.

Does the Orthodox Church of today in fact correspond to the picture we get of the congregation of the Apostolic Age when we read the New Testament and the writings of the Apostolic Fathers? It does — as much as a grown-up person corresponds to a picture taken of him as a child. Although the Church has developed, it is the same in essence and spirit in the twentieth century as it has been from the beginning.

The coming of Christ when the time was "fulfilled" (Mk 1:15) was an appointed event; indeed, our calendar begins there. The outpouring of the Holy Spirit in fulfilment of the "promise of the Father" (Acts 1:4) was also an appointed, unique historical event. For the Church it meant "power from on high" and "the Spirit of truth" (Lk 24:49, Jn 16:13). On the strength of this we believe that although the grace of the Holy Spirit is at work in the later churches and communities according to their faith, the plenitude of grace once given to the Church in the historical outpouring of the Holy Spirit will not be given again. In a hymn for Pentecost the Church sings:

Blessed art Thou, O Christ our God, who hast revealed the fishermen as most wise by sending down upon them the Holy Spirit; through them Thou didst draw the world into Thy net. O Lover of man, glory to Thee!

"When the Spirit of truth comes He will guide you into all the truth," Christ promised (Jn 16:13). After this promise had been fulfilled, the Apostle indeed gave to the "Church of the living God" the name "pillar and bulwark of the truth" (1 Tim 3:15).

The promised gift of "all the truth" came to the Church in the outpouring of the Holy Spirit, but it took centuries, the whole Patristic Age, to define it using man's limited concepts. And although the Fathers were learned men, profound thinkers, and pure in their lives, this alone is not enough to guarantee the absolute character of the truth inherited from the time of the Fathers. Therefore we need the power of the Holy Spirit, which was given to the Church, to guide it to the truth and to protect it. The verbal formulations of the faith which was in the consciousness of the Church from the very beginning have developed over a long period. Similarly, the whole ecclesiastical life has found richer and richer expressions in the various parts of Christ's Church which differ from one another in form but not in spirit. Thus every attempt to create an apostolic congregation, disregarding the work of the Holy Spirit which has gone on in the Church for two thousand years, seems artificial from the Church's point of view.

Just as Christ has both a divine and a human nature, so has the Church. On its human side the Church is susceptible to errors, weaknesses and failings, but it has consolation in the promise: "I will build my church, and the gates of hell shall not prevail against it." (Mt 16:18) This means that though the storms of time may ravage the human substance of the Church, they will not destroy the Church. The Church will endure until the next period of God's rule over the world is ushered in, until the *parousia* or Second

Coming of Christ. Until then the Church which was established at the first Christian Pentecost will endure as the protector of the truth, maintaining its characteristic features of apostolic priesthood, the Eucharist and other sacraments, and the common experience of the Church, its Tradition.

SOURCES OF DOCTRINE

The sources of doctrine as defined in the Orthodox Catechism are the Holy Bible and the Holy Tradition transmitted by the Church.

Why is the Church given priority as the subject of the first chapter in this book? Because the Church came into being first, and only afterwards, little by little, did the books of the New Testament, the Gospels and Epistles appear. Moreover, when we take into account how few "books," or manuscripts, there were in those days, and the fact that besides the genuine writings there were other gospels and texts written under the names of the Apostles, it is easy to understand how important the living Tradition of the Church was in safeguarding the true Christian faith. The prime importance of Tradition is plainly shown by the fact that it was not until the fifth century that the Church established conclusively which books in circulation should be regarded as genuinely inspired by God's revelation. Thus the Church itself determined the composition of the Bible.

It is to the Church, which defined what the contents of the Bible would be, that the Orthodox Christian turns for his interpretation of the Bible. It is not merely a question of the authority of the Church; the promise was given only to the pure in heart that "they shall see God." (Mt 5:8) In other words, the truths contained in God's word are revealed to a man in the right light only insofar as his heart is purified. No individual person has possessed complete purity of heart and hence complete infallibility in interpreting the word of God. However, this gift has been granted to the Church as a whole through the Spirit of truth acting within it. In practice this means that when all or most of the Church Fathers known for their holy lives have been consistent with one another in their explanation of some point of Scripture, it has become truth to the members of the Church. Without such a criterion the authority of the Bible would rest upon the subjective opinion of each individual trying to interpret it. It is our belief that the Bible by itself, without the Tradition as its living interpreter, is insufficient as a source of truth.

The fifteenth chapter of Acts tells of a meeting held by the Apostles, who announced their decision by saying: "It has seemed good to the Holy Spirit and to us . . ." Similar gatherings of the Apostles' successors, all the bishops of the Church, were held from time to time during the first millennium. At these meetings articles of faith were formulated and decisions made on contemporary problems arising in the life of the Church. Seven such ecclesiastical councils have been recognized by the Church as general or ecumenical and their decisions thus recognized as binding upon the whole Church. The first of these synods or councils was held at Nicaea in the year 325 and the seventh in Constantinople in 787.

In addition to the councils recognized as ecumenical, there have been a number of local councils which were important for the whole Church, in both the first and second millennia. For example, a church council was held in Constantinople in 1351 which confirmed the practice of hesychasm, or unceasing prayer of the heart, together with the teaching of St. Gregory Palamas on the uncreated light of the Holy Spirit.

Since the 1960's the local Orthodox Churches have been making preparations for a common council or so-called Great and Holy Synod whose purpose will be to find solutions to the new problems confronting the Church today.

History shows that in the past, meetings which had the authority of Ecumenical Councils have always been called together in the face of a threat to the unity and truth of the Church. Among such threats, for instance, were the

Christological heresies concerning the nature of Christ. In our own time the acute problem awaiting a common solution is the so-called diaspora problem, which is weakening the Orthodox witness in the world. In our century the Church has outgrown its own historical garment, so to speak; it has spread over new continents so that it is no longer only the Eastern Church but is Western just as well. This situation calls for recognition of the independence of the new local Churches which have sprung up, especially in America, so that they may participate fully in the common affairs of the Orthodox Churches. Unlike the Roman Catholic Church, the Orthodox Church has no common administrative center; each of the local Churches whose independence has been recognized has its own independent voice in the common affairs of the Church. For historical reasons the Patriarch of Constantinople holds a position of honour among his peers, but he has no authority over the other independent, or autocephalous, Churches.

In Orthodoxy it is emphasized that doctrine and life are two sides of the same thing. Future general councils of the Church will not be concerned with any new doctrines beyond what "the Fathers have decided," but rather with adapting accepted principles of the Church to changing circumstances. This task presupposes a unity of love and peace among the representatives of the Orthodox Churches, who at the Ecumenical Councils included all the bishops of all the Churches, in order that unanimous decisions may be confirmed with the apostolic seal: "It seemed good to the Holy Spirit and to us."

SALVATION

What is salvation, which is so much talked about but can be interpreted in so many different ways?

Let us start with the words of the Apostle: "all have sinned and fall short of the glory of God." (Rom 3:23) Sin, as violation of God's will, separates man from God, from His glory, and thus brings its own punishment.

God accepts fallen man, however, for he was ransomed not "with silver or gold, but with the precious blood of Christ." (1 Pet 1:18-19)

Nevertheless, acceptance and redemption do not imply a general absolution granted to all mankind, but rather an opportunity given to each person individually to ask for mercy and receive forgiveness for his sins. This is in conformity with the gift of free will given to man.

The part played by man's free will in salvation was shown at Calvary in the different fates of the two evildoers who were crucified with Christ. One of them, the Gospel tells us, "railed at him." The other one repented of his sins and prayed: "Jesus, remember me when you come into your kingdom." In answer he was promised: "Truly I say to you, today you will be with me in Paradise." (Lk 23:39-43) Christ's death brought forgiveness and acceptance to the malefactor who repented.

The different fates of the crucified evildoers and the decisive role of repentance in man's salvation are indicated in the form of a cross known in Karelia: one end of the slanting bar points upwards, to Paradise, and the other downwards, to perdition.

In the service for Friday of Holy Week, between Gospel readings about the passion of Christ, a hymn is sung which is listened to with special devotion:

The wise thief Thou didst make worthy of Paradise in a single moment, O Lord; enlighten me also, through the wood of Thy Cross, and save me.

The evildoer hanging on the cross repented at the last moment, and what remained unfinished after his conversion was completed by Christ's redemptive death. But in the case of those who remain in this life, repentance must be followed by amendment of their ways. Following his very first sermon, St. Peter's listeners asked, "What shall we do?" "Repent," St. Peter replied, "and be baptized every one of you in the name of Jesus Christ for the forgiveness of your sins, and you shall receive the gift of the Holy Spirit." (Acts 2:37-38)

This happens all the time. In Holy Baptism a man is born anew "of water and the Spirit." This is followed by walking "in newness of life" (Rom 6:4) towards the given goal to "be holy yourselves in all your conduct." (1 Pet 1:15)

Although sin has corrupted human nature, man still bears within him the image of God, albeit tarnished by sin. In becoming man, Christ "emptied himself, taking the form of a servant, being born in the likeness of men." (Phil 2:5-8) He became like us men in order to make us, in turn, "partakers of the divine nature." (2 Pet 1:4) Thus Christ became our Saviour not only because "upon Him was the chastisement that made us whole" (Isaiah 53:5) but also because "His divine power granted to us all things that pertain to life and godliness." (2 Pet 1:3) In other words, Christ does not only offer us the forgiveness of our sins, but He also gives His Divine power for our use and for our development so that we might not be "ineffective or unfruitful in the knowledge of our Lord Jesus Christ." (2 Pet 1:8)

In the services before Christmas the following line occurs repeatedly in the hymns: "Christ shall be born, raising the likeness that fell of old," restoring the tarnished image of God in man to its original brightness.

Thus our salvation begins when we receive forgiveness for our sins in Holy Baptism, and indeed many times again later in Confession, the sacrament of repentance or washing with tears. This is followed by new efforts, renewed through the Holy Spirit, to live in Christ as a member of His Body, the Church. The goal of this life is to try to be pure in heart and so to "see God" (Mt 5:8) in the Holy Spirit.

According to a formulation by Bishop Theophan the Recluse, we are saved "by the good will of the Father through the merits of the Son by the grace of the Holy Spirit." It is peculiar to Orthodox services that nearly all of the prayers end with praise to the Holy Trinity: Father, Son, and Holy Spirit.

FAITH AND GOOD WORKS

There is no problem of "faith and good works" in the spirituality of the Church. The relationship between faith and good works becomes a "problem" only when justification is understood as an outward legal process between God and man. In that case people either fear that good deeds will come between the soul and Christ or, on the contrary, they regard deeds as merits in the eyes of God. In the Orthodox view deeds are not an end in themselves for the doer, but are more like a saving instrument in the transformation of man's corrupted nature into a "new creation." (2 Cor 5:17) Therefore Christ's gospel commandments are not law but grace and mercy. They are like medicine given for our use, without which we cannot get well. Let us think of any virtue recommended to us in the Gospel: humility, for instance. How else could we grow in humility except by really humbling ourselves in practice? A prayer from Psalm 119 is often repeated in church services: "Blessed art Thou, O Lord; teach me Thy statutes!"

Because of man's corrupted nature, he has no other way of showing gratitude and love towards Christ than by trying to fulfil in his life the commandments which Christ has given, which work towards his own salvation. "If you love me, you will keep my commandments." (Jn 14:15) The fulfilment of these commandments of Christ which are contained in the Gospels, such as prayer, fasting, serving one's neighbour, humility and refraining from condemning anyone else, can be seen as the leaves of the spiritual tree. The gifts of the Spirit, which are love, joy, peace, patience, kindness, goodness, faithfulness, gentleness and self-control, correspond to the fruits of the tree. (Gal 5:22) They are the signs of a purified heart. The wisdom and difficulty of the spiritual pilgrimage lie in the fact that the leaves must not be regarded as fruits nor yet can one imagine that one can bear fruit without leaves; one cannot acquire the gifts of the Spirit without effort.

SPIRITUAL GUIDANCE

The spiritual struggle of a Christian has never been easy. He has to contend not only against the obvious temptations of the world and against the corruption in himself, not only "against flesh and blood, but against . . . the spiritual hosts of wickedness in the heavenly places." (Eph 6:12)

In addition to the decisive support which participation in the life of the Church offers him, he is comforted by the knowledge that there exists a "great cloud of witnesses," those who have already been through the same struggles and know how to advise and encourage people who follow in their footsteps. The spiritual experience of numerous ascetics is contained in crystallized form in the writings of the Fathers. We can draw on their spiritual wisdom when it is hard to find living examples and guides for the spiritual life, as is the case in our time.

Humble enjoyment of the teachings of the Fathers, whether in the monastic cell of an elder or through books, is a basic part of Orthodox devotional life. "He who has learned obedience," the Fathers advise, "will himself be heard and will enter boldly into the presence of the Crucified One," for the Crucified Lord Himself was "obedient unto death." (Phil 2:8)

THE COMMUNION OF SAINTS

In their spiritual care of each another Christians also rely on intercessory prayers. They ask for one another's prayers and believe that "the prayer of a righteous man has great power in its effects." (Jas 5:16) But life continues after death. It would be strange to think that the prayers of a devout Christian reach God during his temporal life in this world, but not afterwards when he has "departed and is with Christ." (Phil 1:23) Indeed epitaphs from the time of the martyrs show that from the very beginning of Christianity those who have departed into the kingdom of God have been asked to pray for those left behind.

The more deeply a Christian comes to know his own soul and the brighter he is illuminated by the grace of the Holy Spirit, the more deeply he also sees his own sinfulness and its opposite, the greatness of the mercy and love of God. Thus compassionate love towards all human souls fettered by sin grows in him, and prayer for them takes an ever greater place in his life. If this is the case during man's sojourn in the world of time, how much more reason there is for his prayer to continue when he has gone to the kingdom of glory. According to the vision of St. John, there "the smoke of the incense rose with the prayers of the saints from the hand of the angel before God." (Rev 8:4)

There is a constant communion of prayer between the visible, earthly part of the Church, and the invisible, heavenly part, and indeed each day of the year is dedicated to the memory of some saints whose names are known. The stories of their struggles are told in hymns dedicated to them and they are asked to make intercession. Thus we follow the Apostle's exhortation: "Remember your leaders, those who spoke to you the word of God; consider the outcome of their life, and imitate their faith." (Heb 13:7)

In glorifying the saints' spiritual struggle and victory, the Church is in fact glorifying God's work of salvation, the work of the Holy Spirit; it experiences the salvation already accomplished in them, the goal towards which the members of the Church militant are still pressing on. (Phil 3:12, 14)

First among the saints and always to be praised is Mary, the Favoured One, the ever Virgin Mother of God. (Luke 1:28, 48) In her, in St. John the Baptist and in the Apostle John, all of whom led celibate lives, as well as in their countless followers, virginity was restored to the honour which naturally belonged to it before the Fall. (Gen 2:25) Thus one alternative Christian way is to monastic asceticism, which is for those who have received a calling to this way of life. (Mt 19:11-12; 1 Cor 7:7)

The veneration of the saints and our communion with them in prayer are the Church's living experience. For those who lack this experience, it is hard to understand the communion of saints as a communion of prayer. It may indeed depend simply on their good will whether they refrain from claiming that the Orthodox are worshippers of Mary, the saints and the icons; in other words, from bearing false witness against their neighbours. The Church has never adored any other than the Holy Trinity: Father, Son, and Holy Spirit. The saints, as well as all the sacred things through which Divine grace is communicated to man, are venerated, not adored.

II The Eucharist

Serve the Lord with fear, and rejoice in Him with trembling.

Ps 2:11

SERVING GOD

In the previous part we discussed doctrinal themes, not the doctrine as a whole, but a few characteristic features of the early Church which have been cherished by Orthodoxy and which, though natural and self-evident to the Orthodox themselves, may seem peculiar in Protestant surroundings. We turn now to the question of what the Church means to us in practice, how we participate in its life.

When an individual member of the Church is mentioned in the prayers of the Church he is called "the servant of God so-and-so." In the widest sense, serving God, fulfilling God's will, is a man's whole life, but in particular it is the life of prayer, whether in the privacy of one's own room or in corporate worship. A person participates with his whole being in serving God, so that the Apostle's hope may be fulfilled in him: "May the God of peace himself sanctify you wholly; and may your spirit and soul and body be kept sound and blameless at the coming of our Lord Jesus Christ." (1 Thess 5:23)

The practice of private prayer will be the subject of the third part of the book; the aim of this part is to describe how God is served in the congregation, especially in connection with Eucharistic worship. However, let us first look at some general features of Orthodox worship.

When we enter an Orthodox church we notice that the people stand and usually there are just a few seats for those who for some reason are unable to stand. Standing in church is the most natural position for prayer. It is one way, a symbolic way, of showing reverence for God. Man's life is full of symbols as agreed forms of behaviour, not only in the religious sphere but elsewhere as well.

The sign of the Cross which we see people making is one of the oldest Christian symbols. In Orthodox worship people make the sign of the Cross at special moments in the service, and at other times as well, according to their own feeling in prayer. The sign of the Cross is a wordless confession of faith: the thumb and first two fingers of the right hand joined together symbolize our belief in the Holy Trinity, and the other two fingers pressed against the palm represent our belief that the Saviour was both God and man. The sign of the Cross, kneeling and prostrations give expression to the thoughts of the worshipper and to the feelings in his heart. But at the same time these outward gestures affect him inwardly, strengthening the right frame of mind in him. They also help a person who is weaker in prayer to enter more fully into the spirit of the common prayer of the Church.

We shall see that many other symbols too are used in services. Thus when the priest gives a blessing either with his hand or with the Cross, the congregation bow their heads to receive the blessing. The smoke of the incense, according to the psalm, symbolizes prayer rising before the face of God. The candles which worshippers place in front of the icons express fervent prayer.

The services include reading and singing. The reading is done in a recitative or singing voice. This way of reading shows that the celebrant is not expressing his own feelings, but the common prayer of the Church, in which it is easy for all to join. The corporate character of the prayer is particularly important. Many of the prayers used in the Church are Biblical texts or are otherwise inherited from the early Church. The songs too are prayer: praise, thanksgiving, supplication, proclamation. Sung prayer is always the common prayer of the Church. Therefore it is always the text of the song which is most important, directing the thoughts and hearts of the worshippers to the same subject of prayer. Instrumental music is not used in Orthodox worship, for each listener experiences it in his own way. Church songs with their texts and melodies are regarded as an organic part of the service. For this reason genuine liturgical music based on tradition is of the greatest value. Along with choral singing, congregational singing is fundamental, especially in the Liturgy.

During a service the congregation, under the leadership of the bishop or priest, participates in certain activities according to the established pattern of the service. The pattern of the service dates back to the early Church and varies according to the time of day and the church year. Thus there is Vespers in the evening, with which the church day begins, Compline before bed, the Midnight Office, Matins in the morning, and the Hours throughout the day. The most central service is the one in which the sacrament of Holy Communion is celebrated. This service is called the Liturgy, or Eucharist.

A person who is not a member of the Orthodox Church may attend an Orthodox service. The visitor may stand in the church like the others without being noticed. But if he wishes he may also participate in the service and express his prayer in the same symbols as the Orthodox. The one thing which only members of the Orthodox Church can participate in is Holy Communion. Why this is so will become clear in the following chapters when we take a closer look at the Eucharist from the point of view of the individual Christian as well as that of the whole Church.

THE SACRAMENT OF OUR REDEMPTION

That remarkable teacher in the early Church in the West, the blessed Augustine, speaks of his mother, the pious Monica, in his *Confessions* as follows:

She only desired to be remembered at Thy altar, which she had served without ever missing so much as a day. For she knew that at Thy altar we receive the holy Victim Who cancelled the decree that was against us and in Whom we have triumphed over the enemy who reckons up our sins, tries to find some charge against us, and yet can find no fault in Him in Whom we conquer ... To this sacrament of our redemption Thy handmaid had bound her soul by the bond of faith. (IX:13)

This testimony of Augustine concerning his mother, who had "bound her soul to the sacrament of redemption by the bond of faith," tells us something very essential about the faith of a Christian, something that was important not only in Monica's time in the early Church of the fourth century, but even today.

The visible centre of the spiritual life of the individual member of the Church as well as that of the whole Church is still the Holy Altar and the sacrament of redemption which is performed there. This sacrament is called Holy Communion, and the service in which it takes place is called the Holy and Divine Liturgy.

Participation in Holy Communion is the physical aspect of this sacrament of our redemption, but its audible and verbal content is the offering of thanksgiving—*eucharistia* in Greek — to God the Father. In this verbal service the main cause for thanksgiving is the redemptive sacrifice once offered by Christ for the sake of mankind; the Eucharist is also called a bloodless sacrifice of thanksgiving.

In the early Church, according to Augustine, the Christian bound his soul to the sacrament of redemption simply by the bond of faith. For us today, however, it is necessary to make a deliberate effort to enter deeply into the subject before the fundamental significance of this sacrament becomes clear to us. We must hasten to add, however, that not even the most thorough knowledge about this sacrament can change its suprarational, hidden character. Hence in the Orthodox Church Holy Communion, and the other sacraments as well, are called mysteries. In the text of the Liturgy participation in the Holy Mysteries means participation in the Eucharist and in Communion.

THE LITURGY AS A BAPTISMAL FEAST

In the first centuries it was most usual for people to become members of the Church as adults. A person received baptism and became a member of the Church after he had learned the truths of the faith. In practice this instruction of catechumens, people preparing for baptism, took place mainly in connection with the Holy Liturgy. But those preparing for baptism were allowed to be present only during the first part of the Liturgy. Still today this part of the Liturgy is called the Liturgy of the Catechumens. Its central feature is the scriptural reading and the teaching, or sermon. After hearing the Word explained, the catechumens took part in prayers offered on their behalf. These included petitions to "make them worthy in due time of the laver of regeneration," or baptism, and to "unite them to Thy Holy, Catholic and Apostolic Church." Then, after receiving the bishop's blessing, the catechumens departed from the service. Only the faithful who had already been baptized could remain in the church, and hence the second part of the Liturgy is still called the Liturgy of the Faithful.

This preparation for baptism in connection with the Liturgy usually went on throughout the six weeks of Lent. Then on Great Saturday or Easter Day itself the catechumens were led into the baptistry or to a shore where they were baptized. From there the newly baptized together with the whole congregation walked in solemn procession into the church. In the church the bishop laid his hands upon the newly baptized or — in later practice — anointed them with holy chrism as a sign of the gift of the Holy Spirit. Having thus become members of the Church, the newly baptized could now be present for the first time at the Liturgy of the Faithful, participating in the Eucharist and receiving Holy Communion.

From what has been said it is clear that preparation for baptism was not only a matter of learning the articles of Christian belief theoretically, but also an important part of it consisted in gradually beginning to participate in the liturgical life of the Church, entering into its spirit and thus really "binding one's soul to the sacrament of redemption by the bond of faith."

THE EASTER OF THE BAPTIZED

Baptism is participation in Christ's death and resurrection. The Apostle writes about it in this way: "We were buried therefore with Him by baptism into death, so that as Christ was raised from the dead by the glory of the Father, we too might walk in newness of life." (Rom 6:3-4)

Easter as the baptismal feast as such went out of use in the Eastern Church as early as the eleventh century, but its most distinctive features still survive in the Easter service. As in the past, when the congregation carrying lighted candles walked in procession with the newly baptized from the place of baptism to the church, so now on Easter night the Christians go in procession around the church as if it were their common baptismal feast.

Then, when the tidings of Christ's resurrection have been proclaimed for the first time at the entrance of the church, we step from the darkness into a church flooded with light. There, as Matins begins, we hear the singing of the Easter canon, in which our baptism is referred to as if it had just taken place:

Yesterday I was buried with Thee, O Christ: Today I rise with Thee in Thy resurrection. Yesterday I was crucified with Thee: Do Thou glorify me with Thee in Thy kingdom.

And soon, as the Liturgy begins, we are again reminded of our baptism in the song: "As many of you as have been baptized into Christ have put on Christ. Alleluia!"

Baptism is the most decisive event in our lives. But how little attention it has received! Participation in the Feast of the Resurrection, our common baptismal feast, is a vivid reminder of how "we too might walk in newness of life." And what is that newness of life which is present at the Easter Feast? We experience it when we take part in the Eucharist. Thus it is most natural and important that all baptized members of the Church should partake of Holy Communion also, and most particularly in the Liturgy of Easter night.

THROUGH THE LITURGY INTO THE CHURCH

Nowadays people become members of the Church in infancy through holy baptism. Holy Communion too is received in infancy. Hence entering into the spirit of the Holy Liturgy and conscious participation in the sacrament of redemption depend at first on the child's parents and godparents, on the strength of whose faith the child has been baptized. The practical instruction given at home while a small child is taken to Communion in church is continued later in religion classes at school.

Because Communion is received in infancy, the Orthodox Church does not hold confirmation classes as such, but it has classes of a similar nature for young people. One important task in these classes as well as in those at school is to teach everything about the Liturgy that the early Church taught in preparation for baptism.

An adult wishing to join the Orthodox Church can prepare for it as was done in the early Church, by making himself familiar with the liturgical life of the Church. This is in fact what usually does happen. As he attends church he first gets acquainted with the services and learns to take part in them. Then "in due time" — as the prayer for the catechumens puts it — God's grace will awaken in him the desire to be able to share in the Eucharistic community of the faithful. This sharing is made possible — provided that he has already been baptized — through the sacrament of chrismation. Because it signifies joining the Church, the *ecclesia*, chrismation should be conferred, as it was in the early Church, in connection with the Liturgy, when the Church is concretely present as a congregation, as a gathered Eucharistic community.

The baptismal practice of the early Church helps us to

understand that the baptism of an infant, his becoming a member of the Church, is not a private occasion for the home either, but it is explicitly a feast common to the whole congregation. When a child is baptized in church during the Liturgy we experience even in our day how baptism and the receiving of the gift of the Holy Spirit make a person a member of the people of God. The newly baptized child — like the adult who joins the Church, as mentioned above — can then already, in the same Liturgy, partake of the sacrament of redemption, Holy Communion, the fulfilment of all spiritual longing.

RECEIVING COMMUNION

"The divine liturgy is truly a heavenly service on earth," wrote John of Kronstadt, a priest who lived at the beginning of this century and had received the power of healing and spiritual vision. He himself celebrated the Liturgy every day.

The heavenly repast is laid before us and we hear Christ's own words inviting: *Take! Eat! This is My Body . . . Drink of it, all of you! This is My Blood . . .*[1]

Can there be any doubt that these words urge us all to receive Holy Communion in every Liturgy! In the early Church only the unbaptized and the so-called penitents, who had been excluded from Communion because of grave sins, did not partake of the Holy Gifts. But they did not hear Christ's invitation, because they had to leave before the beginning of the Liturgy of the Faithful. On the other hand, it was quite unthinkable that those who stayed for the Liturgy of the Faithful should have abstained from Communion. Only gradually, with the cooling of the Christians' love, did it begin to be customary for only some of the church members present — or even only the celebrating clergy — to receive Communion.

In our time the liturgical movement, which began in the Western Churches after the First World War, has been seeking a return to early Christian liturgical practice. Thus the Liturgy of the Orthodox Church, as the preserver of the oldest Christian tradition, has become the object of special attention. At the same time the Orthodox themselves

---

[1] In this and the following chapters, words printed in italic are quoted from *The Divine Liturgy according to St. John Chrysostom* (trans. Orthodox Church in America, Second Edition, St. Tikhon's Seminary Press, 1977).

have had to re-examine the traditions preserved by their Church. This in turn has led to the revival of the early Christian practice of regular communion in many places within the Orthodox Church, especially in the West.

In the Finnish Orthodox Church too the bishops' pastoral letter of 1970 emphasizes the original meaning of the Liturgy. The letter explains that the sacraments of confession and Communion are not bound together in such a way that confession is a necessary condition for admission to Communion. In practice it may be regarded as a "condition" only when a person seldom goes to Communion, for instance only "at least once a year," as unfortunately used to be taught as a kind of rule. But a person who receives Communion frequently goes to confession only when he feels a special need for it or during Lent, a general time for repentance and examination of the direction of our lives.

There can be no absolute rules about going to confession, but the bishops' pastoral letter urges each person to consult his own confessor and receive his blessing for frequent Communion. However, everyone should try to make absence from Communion the exception rather than the rule.

Augustine's mother Monica received the sacrament of the altar every day. This is not possible for us, because here the Liturgy is celebrated daily only in monasteries. However, the practice described in the New Testament is possible for us too. The Christians used to meet regularly on the first day of the week for the "breaking of bread," or to celebrate the Eucharist. This day was called the Lord's Day, because it was the day of Christ's resurrection. On that day, Sunday, we too have a Liturgy in all our congregations, and nothing should be allowed to prevent us from receiving the sacrament of redemption as a whole family in the Liturgy on the Lord's Day.

The sabbath used to be celebrated to glorify the act of

creation. Through Christ's resurrection death was overcome, and so creation was restored to its original glory. This is why Sunday, the first day of the week, has supplanted the sabbath; and the people of God, the Christians, assemble to meet their Risen Lord.

UNTO LIFE, NOT UNTO CONDEMNATION

Christ speaks about the importance of Communion: "Unless you eat the flesh of the Son of man and drink his blood, you have no life in you; he who eats my flesh and drinks my blood has eternal life, and I will raise him up at the last day." (Jn 6:53-54)

On hearing these words the Jews were offended. We know what is meant. "Life in us," the real life of faith, is possible only "in Christ," in the real communion with Christ which is realized in Holy Communion. And this communion will continue until the day of resurrection: "and I will raise him up at the last day." This is an amazing mystery, which makes a person long for Holy Communion, especially when death is approaching.

Regular Communion has already become customary in many of our parishes. However, we must always remember the Apostle's warning: "For any one who eats and drinks without discerning the body eats and drinks judgment upon himself." (1 Cor 11:29)

Although it is not necessary to go to confession before Communion every time, nevertheless we must prepare ourselves every time to meet the Risen Christ in Communion. This preparation includes fasting: in the morning before going to the Liturgy we must not eat or drink anything. In the Orthodox prayer book there is a small rule of prayer, a few prayers which are meant to be read at home before going to church for Communion. A prayerful mind has a transforming effect upon the body as well, so that the slight hunger which the body feels is changed to a spiritual hunger for communion with God, and to a sense of expectation. Such preparations awaken the mood of humility and repentance which is appropriate for approaching the sacrament and about which the Apostle says: "Let a man examine himself, and so eat of the bread and drink of the cup." (1 Cor 11:28)

Let no one, however, because of his unworthiness, fail to accept the Lord's invitation heard in the Liturgy, or think that by receiving Communion less often he can prepare for it better and be more worthy. The sense of unworthiness is just the right mood, the only one which permits us to be sharers in God's supreme grace offered to us as a completely free gift.

Anyone who has the opportunity for quiet after going home from church can also read in his prayer book the prayers of thanksgiving after Communion.

THE LITURGY — COMMON WORSHIP

Thus far we have spoken about the Holy Liturgy as a service in which we receive Holy Communion, the medicine of immortality, as it was called by the Apostolic Fathers. But at the same time the Liturgy is much more than spiritual medicine for individual church members. The very name liturgy — borrowed from the Greek — means public service.

In the Liturgy the Church fulfills itself; only then is it the *ecclesia* gathered in one place for common action and service. The reason for this coming together and its purpose may be deduced from the following words of the Apostle:

And like living stones be yourselves built into a spiritual house, to be a holy priesthood, to offer spiritual sacrifices acceptable to God through Jesus Christ . . .

But you are a chosen race, a royal priesthood, a holy nation, God's own people, that you may declare the wonderful deeds of him who called you out of darkness into his marvellous light. Once you were no people but now you are God's people; once you had not received mercy, but now you have received mercy. (1 Pet 2:5; 9-10)

These words of the Apostle indicate that terms formerly applied to Israel now belong to the new Israel, to the Christians, the *ecclesia,* the Church. Whereas previously only Aaron's family had been chosen to serve as priests, now the new Israel as a whole, all the members of the Church, are a chosen, holy family, a royal priesthood and God's own people. As a holy priesthood they are all called to "offer spiritual sacrifices acceptable to God through Jesus Christ."

This bringing of spiritual offerings is just what takes

place in the Holy Liturgy, which the whole people of God performs as a common service. All the prayers of the Holy Liturgy, with a very few exceptions, are in the plural, and thus intended to be read or sung in the name of the whole people of God. An example of this is one of the Prayers of the Antiphons in the first part of the Liturgy:

O Thou who hast given us grace with one accord to make our common supplications unto Thee, and hast promised that when two or three are gathered together in Thy name Thou wouldst grant their requests: Fulfill now, O Lord, the petitions of Thy servants as may be expedient for them: granting us in this world the knowledge of Thy truth, and in the world to come, life everlasting. For Thou art a good God and lovest mankind, and unto Thee we ascribe glory: to the Father, and to the Son, and to the Holy Spirit, now and ever and unto ages of ages.

In the early Church all the prayers of the Liturgy were read aloud. The whole congregation participated in them. But as early as the sixth century some of the prayers of the Liturgy began to be read in a low voice by the celebrating priest. Although there were attempts to oppose this change, it gradually became the general practice, so that the handbook still indicates which parts of the prayers in the Liturgy are to be read "secretly," by the priest alone. However, insofar as there has been an effort to deepen the congregation's understanding of the Liturgy, it has now been found necessary to go back to the practice of reading the prayers of the Liturgy aloud.

How can the whole assembly of God's people participate in the sacrament of redemption with full understanding and true feeling and realize that they are a royal priesthood bringing spiritual offerings, if they hear only fragments or closing sentences of the common prayers without being aware of their meaning as a whole? As this is still most often the case, the people present can only follow the service without any other support than their own personal mood of prayer or else remain a more or less distracted audience. In the latter case people tend to pay special attention to the outward, aesthetical side of the Liturgy, and indulge in admiring the splendour of the service and the fine singing. It is true that these aspects, reflecting the heavenly glory of God, have their own value, but only as a framework for the content of the Eucharist. They must not become ends in themselves. The early Church lacked any outward splendour; Eucharistic solemnity was found in the joyous encounter with the Risen Christ.

Christ himself is the celebrant of the Liturgy. This is made clear in the prayer read by the priest before the Cherubic Hymn. This prayer differs from other prayers in the Liturgy in that it is the personal prayer of the celebrating priest, in which he asks for strength to perform the sacrament. By praying in this way the priest acknowledges that it is Christ himself who offers the *liturgical and bloodless sacrifice* which has been committed to the priest: *For Thou art the Offerer and the Offered, the Receiver and the Received, O Christ our God.* Christ acts through the priest, however. Just as Christ celebrated Communion, gave thanks, blessed, broke, and gave to His disciples, so too in the Liturgy the celebrant always performs the holy sacrament, but he does it as the voice of the whole people of God and with them. He gives thanks, reading the Eucharistic prayers of thanksgiving, blesses, breaks and gives to the people; all the others are his co-celebrants, each in his own place: the other priests and deacons standing around the altar and all the other members of the people of God in the church.

The people standing in the church are not passive attenders but are co-celebrants with the officiating priest or bishop, and they must be able to follow the course of the Liturgy and participate in its prayers. Only in this way can the Liturgy be real liturgy — common worship — and the Church an *ecclesia* — the people of God assembled for the Eucharist.

THE EUCHARIST — A SACRIFICE OF THANKSGIVING

In the preceding chapter we quoted the words of the Apostle Peter referring to the sacrificial nature of the Liturgy: "Be yourselves built into a spiritual house, to be a holy priesthood, to offer spiritual sacrifices to God through Jesus Christ."

This is realized in the most central part of the Liturgy of the Faithful, the Eucharist proper. There, in the Anaphora, or prayers of offering through words spoken by the priest, the congregation as a spiritual priesthood makes a bloodless spiritual offering, giving thanks to God for all that He has done for mankind. Our first thanks are for His having *brought us from nonexistence into being.* We go on to thank Him because *when we had fallen away He raised us up again . . . and endowed us with His Kingdom which is to come.* Thanksgiving is addressed to the Holy Trinity *for all things of which we know and of which we know not, whether manifest or unseen* that God has done for us. Especially we offer thanks for *this Liturgy which He has deigned to accept at our hands, though there stand by Him thousands of archangels . . . singing the triumphant hymn, shouting, proclaiming and saying: Holy! Holy! Holy! . . .*

The whole congregation joins in the prayer, singing:

Holy! Holy! Holy! Lord of Sabaoth! Heaven and earth are full of Thy glory! Hosanna in the highest! Blessed is He that comes in the name of the Lord! Hosanna in the highest!

Thus joining in the singing of the heavenly choirs the congregation acknowledges the sanctity and glory of God who so loved His *world as to give His Only-begotten Son,*

*that whoever believes in Him should not perish but have
everlasting life. For He — in the night in which He gave
Himself for the life of the world — took bread . . . and when
He had given thanks and blessed it, and hallowed it, and
broken it, He gave it to His holy disciples and apostles
saying:*

*Take! Eat! This is My Body which is broken for you,
for the remission of sins.*

And likewise, after supper, He took the cup, saying:

*Drink of it, all of you! This is My Blood of the New
Testament, which is shed for you and for many, for the
remission of sins!* Remembering this *saving commandment*
and the whole mystery of redemption connected with it:
*the Cross, the Tomb, the Resurrection on the third day,
the Ascension into heaven, the Sitting at the right hand, and
second and glorious Coming,* the priest elevates the Holy
Gifts — the bread and the wine in the chalice — which have
been placed upon the Holy Altar, and says:

*Thine own of Thine own we offer unto Thee, on behalf
of all and for all.* Thus offering this *reasonable and bloodless worship* the congregation prays to God: *Send down
Thy Holy Spirit upon us and upon these gifts here offered*
and so make the *Bread the precious Body of Thy Christ*
and what is in the cup *the precious Blood of Thy Christ.*
At the same time the celebrant blesses the Bread and the
Cup, each of them separately and then together. Following
this the clergy and the congregation sing with one voice:
Amen. Amen. Amen.

Thus the people of God, bringing forth or offering the
bread and wine, chosen out of the foods which sustain
earthly life, receives a heavenly repast, the holy Body and
Blood of Christ, for the sustenance of its spiritual life. The
Orthodox Church does not attempt to explain the invisible
yet real change of the bread and wine into the Body and
Blood of Christ, for it is a mystery and is meant to be
received with faith.

St. Ambrose, Bishop of Milan, who lived in the fourth century, wrote a prayer to be read by those preparing to celebrate the Holy Liturgy. The following extracts from the prayer show the early Church's conception of the Holy Eucharist and of its connection with the sacrifice of redemption:

Our true High Priest, Jesus Christ! For us sinners Thou didst offer Thyself on the altar of Thy Cross as a pure sacrifice without blemish. Thou gavest Thy Body for us to eat and Thy Blood for us to drink and didst institute the power of the Holy Spirit, saying: "As often as you do this, do it in remembrance of Me."

I pray to Thee through the high price of our salvation, Thy most precious Blood; I pray to Thee through Thy wonderful and unspeakable love, with which Thou hast so loved us sinners that Thou hast washed us clean from our sins with Thine own Blood, teach me, Thy undeserving servant ... by the power of Thy Spirit to perform this great Sacrament with the reverence and devotion, the piety and fear that befit its worth ...

May Thy Holy Spirit enter my heart and, silently speaking make known the whole truth of this great Mystery so deeply hidden and covered with a Divine veil ...

Furthermore I pray to Thy goodness, O Lord, may the fullness of Thy Divinity come upon this bread; may the invisible form and inconceivable glory of Thy Holy Spirit, O Lord, descend as it did upon the sacrifice of our Fathers of old; may He make the Gifts we offer Thy Body and Blood, and may He guide me, Thy unworthy servant, in performing this great Sacrament ...

UNITY AND ONENESS IN CHRIST

"Do this in remembrance of me" (1 Cor 11:24-25) After this exhortation has been followed in the manner described in the preceding chapter and the Holy Gifts have been blessed, there is a prayer *that they may be to those who partake for the purification of soul, for the remission of sins, for the communion of Thy Holy Spirit, for the fulfillment of the Kingdom of Heaven, for boldness towards Thee, and not for judgment or condemnation.*

The first to be commemorated are the righteous men of the Old Testament who lived in faith in future salvation, then the *apostles, preachers, evangelists, martyrs, confessors, ascetics, and every righteous spirit made perfect in faith* — and first among these the *Theotokos (Mother of God) and ever-virgin Mary*, then John the Baptist, the apostles and the saint on whose day the Liturgy is being celebrated. Then the celebrant commemorates the members of the congregation who have passed away in the hope of eternal life and resurrection.

Then follows commemoration of the living, of the whole world, the whole Church and those in authority, mentioning the bishop of the diocese by name, and also the congregation, especially travellers, the sick and the suffering, captives, those who bring offerings and those who remember the poor. In these prayers one can feel how the sacrament of redemption unites the heavenly triumphant congregation and the militant congregation still struggling in this world.

The celebrant concludes the Anaphora with an exclamation praying that we may praise the Holy Trinity *with one mouth and one heart*, and blesses the people saying: *And the mercies of our great God and Saviour Jesus Christ shall be with all of you.*

THE HOLY THINGS FOR THE HOLY

After the Eucharistic prayers of thanksgiving and commemoration we begin to prepare ourselves to receive Holy Communion. A series of supplications called the Litany of Supplication follows in which we pray for all that is important for our souls. Then the Lord's Prayer is sung, preceded by the prayer: *Make us worthy to partake of the heavenly and awesome Mysteries of this sacred and spiritual table with a pure conscience: for remission of sins, for forgiveness of transgressions, for the communion of the Holy Spirit, for the inheritance of the Kingdom of Heaven, for boldness towards Thee, but not for judgment or condemnation.*

When we have thus prayed that we may with a pure conscience partake of the sacrament of redemption and after we have with boldness approached the God of Heaven as our Father, through the Lord's Prayer, we pray with bowed heads that the Lord may *distribute these Gifts here offered, unto all of us for good, according to the individual need of each . . . through the grace and compassion and love toward mankind of Thine Only-begotten Son.*

Lest anyone's prayer should weaken as he waits to partake of the Holy Gifts, the celebrant utters the words: *The Holy Things for the holy!* At the same time he elevates the Bread, the Lamb, for the people to see, and they respond: *One is Holy! One is the Lord, Jesus Christ, to the glory of God the Father. Amen!* After this exclamation, which is intended to make the believer feel his own dependence on Christ, who alone is holy, the priest breaks the bread, saying: *Divided and distributed is the Lamb of God: who is divided, yet not disunited; who is ever eaten, yet never consumed; but sanctifying those who partake thereof.*

All these prayers are a preparation for receiving Holy Communion. In practice there is often a slackening at this point in the Liturgy, a break in the otherwise continuous course of the Liturgy. Why is this? The altar doors and curtain are closed and the congregation cannot see the clergy in the sanctuary. The choir looks for a song to "fill" the interval before the Royal Doors are opened again. At worst this becomes the moment for a concert, an exhibition of the artistic skill of the choir which completely diverts the thoughts of the listeners from the state of "holy expectation" that has been reached in the Liturgy.

This defect can easily be eliminated: the altar doors should be left open. Since the practice now is to keep them open otherwise throughout the Liturgy, there is no reason why the clergy should separate themselves from the rest of the people of God behind closed doors at this point. Seeing the great devotion with which the clergy partake of Holy Communion will help the people in the church to prepare for the same holy moment. While the clergy are partaking of Holy Communion the choir may sing Psalm 34, but slowly and so quietly that it does not disturb the concentration of those receiving Communion in the sanctuary. And if the Psalm ends before the clergy are ready to continue the Liturgy, the Reader may read some of the prayers of preparation for Communion, but a moment of silence here is equally appropriate.

WITH FAITH AND LOVE DRAW NEAR

After the clergy have partaken of Holy Communion, the faithful are invited to the Lord's Supper: *In the fear of God, and with faith and love, draw near!*

The faithful approach and in a low voice say this prayer along with the celebrating bishop or priest:

I believe, O Lord, and I confess that Thou art truly the Christ, the Son of the living God, who camest into the world to save sinners, of whom I am first. I believe also that this is truly Thine own most pure Body, and that this is truly Thine own precious Blood. Therefore I pray Thee: have mercy upon me and forgive my transgressions both voluntary and involuntary, of word and of deed, committed in knowledge or in ignorance. And make me worthy to partake without condemnation of Thy most pure Mysteries, for the remission of my sins, and unto life everlasting.

Of Thy Mystical Supper, O Son of God, accept me today as a communicant; for I will not speak of Thy Mystery to Thine enemies, neither like Judas will I give Thee a kiss; but like the thief will I confess Thee: Remember me, O Lord, in Thy Kingdom.

May the communion of Thy holy Mysteries be neither to my judgment, nor to my condemnation, O Lord, but to the healing of soul and body.

Then all prostrate themselves and rise again, saying inwardly: "Behold, I come to my immortal King and my God!" Before the holy cup each one says his or her Christian name to the priest, and the priest says: *The servant (handmaid) of God (name), partakes of the precious and holy Body and Blood of our Lord and God and Saviour Jesus Christ, for the remission of sins and unto life everlasting.*

After receiving Communion each one kisses the chalice as representing the pierced side of the Saviour from which blood and water flowed. (Jn 19:34) Then they take some wine mixed with water and a piece of blessed bread, which have been placed on a side table. This, however, is not possible if the number of the communicants is very large.

We do not prostrate ourselves on the day we receive Communion because the Lord's word has come true: "He who eats my flesh and drinks my blood abides in me, and I in him." (Jn 6:56)

When all have partaken of Communion the priest blesses the people saying: *O God, save Thy people, and bless Thine inheritance,* and like an echo of the salvation which the people of God who are present have experienced, they respond with the song:

We have seen the true Light! We have received the heavenly Spirit! We have found the true Faith, worshipping the undivided Trinity, who has saved us!

As the Holy Gifts are removed from the altar they are shown to the people, who hear the priest's words: *Blessed is our God always, now and ever and unto ages of ages.* With these words the last part of the Liturgy begins, a thanksgiving for this participation in the Mysteries of God. Continuing the priest's prayers of thanksgiving, the congregation sings:

Let our mouths be filled with Thy praise, O Lord, that we may sing of Thy glory; for Thou hast made us worthy to partake of Thy holy, divine, immortal and life-creating Mysteries.

And this hymn ends with the supplication: *Keep us in Thy holiness, that all the day we may meditate upon Thy righteousness. Alleluia! Alleluia! Alleluia!* The litany of thanksgiving following this hymn ends with a similar expression of praise: *For Thou art our Sanctification, and unto Thee we ascribe glory: to the Father, and to the Son, and to the Holy Spirit, now and ever and unto ages of ages.*

Then, standing in the midst of the congregation, the priest reads the concluding prayer of the Liturgy, which sums up, as it were, the themes of all the prayers of the Liturgy: *O Lord, who blessest those who bless Thee, and sanctifiest those who trust in Thee: Save Thy people and bless Thine inheritance* ...

The Liturgy concludes with the Lord's blessing and a dismissal, in which are mentioned the names of the saints close to our Church and those commemorated on this day. The faithful go forward to venerate the Cross held in the priest's hand, by kissing this symbol of our redemption.

And so the faithful, having participated in the Holy Eucharist, take the sense of holiness to their homes and into their whole lives, repeating in their minds the prayer: "Keep us in Thy holiness, that all the day we may meditate upon Thy righteousness. Alleluia!"

Thus life moves on from Eucharist to Eucharist towards "the measure of the stature of the fulness of Christ," until we shall see Him "face to face." (Eph 4:13; 1 Cor 13:12)

O Christ! Great and most holy Pascha! O Wisdom, Word, and Power of God! Grant that we may more perfectly partake of Thee in the never-ending Day of Thy Kingdom.

UNTIL HE COMES

"As this broken bread was scattered over the hills and then, when gathered, became one mass, so may Thy Church be gathered from the ends of the earth into Thy Kingdom." (*Didache* 9:4)[1] This beautiful parable of the unity which is realized in the thanksgiving supper, or Eucharist, is used in a first-century literary source called *The Teaching of the Twelve Apostles.* The Eucharist unites "every righteous spirit made perfect in faith" with the members of the Church militant who partake of Christ's holiness and who in the Liturgy are called holy.

"Because there is one bread, we who are many are one body, for we all partake of the one bread." (1 Cor 10:17) The New Testament expression to be "in Christ" has the same meaning as the Apostle's words about one bread and one body: unity of the faith is realized in Christ through the Holy Eucharist. (Rom 12:5; 2 Cor 5:17; Gal 3:28)

So it is also in the life of the congregation. The stronger the sense of Eucharistic, spiritual unity within the congregation, the greater the unanimity, peace and love. Just as all members of one body are equal, so there are neither rich nor poor, high nor low, learned nor uneducated, employers nor labourers, priests nor laymen before the Lord's Cup, but all are redeemed with the same precious Blood and are one in Christ. (Gal 3:29)

The Eucharist, the heart of the life of the Church, also has an eschatological meaning extending to the Second Coming of Christ. "For as often as you eat this bread and

---

[1] *Ancient Christian Writers, The Works of the Fathers in Translation,* vol. 6 (The Mercier Press, Cork, 1948), p. 20.

drink the cup, you proclaim the Lord's death until he comes." (1 Cor 11:26) The Eucharist will be celebrated until the Second Coming of Christ, but this can also be put the other way round. In the Eucharist God's love is met by man's love. However, at the close of the age, when "most men's love will grow cold," (Mt 24:12) the Eucharist will no longer be celebrated, and the time for Christ's Second Coming will have arrived.

THE LITURGY OF THE PRESANCTIFIED

The life of a Christian goes on from Eucharist to Eucharist. Participation in the Sacrament of Redemption on the Lord's Day is the climax of the week. Then the day is really holy: we meet the Risen Lord.

But Sunday is followed by the other days of the week. Early Church history tells us that the Christians felt such a longing to participate in the Lord's Supper that they did not always wait for the next Lord's Day. After the Age of the Martyrs was over and the Church began to enjoy more peaceful times, the practice of celebrating the Liturgy also on other days of the week, especially on Saturdays, on days commemorating martyrs, and on other feasts, was introduced in many places. The story of Monica shows that the Eucharist was celebrated every day.

During Lent the Christians wanted to be strengthened through Holy Communion as often as possible. However, on weekdays in Lent, except Saturday, there was no celebration of the Eucharist, since the Liturgy is always a festal service, not appropriate to fasting days. Thus it became customary to distribute on weekdays the Eucharistic Gifts which had been consecrated in the Liturgy of the previous Lord's Day. This Communion most often took place in a service called the Liturgy of the Presanctified, which was celebrated on Wednesdays and Fridays. The Liturgy of the Presanctified is ascribed to the Roman Pope St. Gregory the Great, the "Dialogist"; the usual Liturgy of the Orthodox Church is associated with the names of St. Basil the Great and St. John Chrysostom.

A special feature of the Liturgy of the Presanctified is that it is celebrated in the evening in connection with Vespers. The early Christians preparing to receive Communion at the Liturgy of the Presanctified fasted the whole day from morning till evening. Today complete fasting is prescribed starting from noon, so that after twelve o'clock we have nothing to eat or drink until after the evening Liturgy.

The evening Liturgies during Lent are important because members of the congregation who work in the daytime are also able to come. Thus as many people as possible can take part in these Lenten services of contrition and hope, and can receive Communion. These evening liturgies renew the early Christian practice of receiving Communion in the evening, which is indicated by the name "Lord's Supper."

III Prayer

> *Continue steadfastly in prayer, being watchful in it with thanksgiving.*
>
> COL 4:2

III Prayer

OUR MISSION

In the previous part we dwelt upon the Eucharist: it is indeed the sanctification of our spiritual and physical lives, the means by which men become "partakers of the divine nature" of Christ.

When we participate in the Eucharist we experience the Kingdom of God here and now. This experience is a foretaste of the holiness of the life to come. But we are still living in this world; our mission continues here. It is a mission assigned to us by God, as we hear in every Eucharistic service: *For as often as you eat this Bread and drink this Cup, you proclaim My Death, you confess My Resurrection!* These words are from the Liturgy of St. Basil the Great. They mean that we today, as God's people gathering for the Eucharist, are continuing the living witness to Christ which has come down from the Apostles. The Apostle writes of this witness: "We saw it, and testify to it, and proclaim to you the eternal life which was with the Father and was made manifest to us." (1 Jn 1:2)

As we leave the Liturgy the words of the hymn follow us: *We have seen the true Light! We have received the Heavenly Spirit! We have found the true Faith ...* This is our mission: to take this Light which we have seen in the Eucharist into the world and to fulfill the Lord's words: "Let your light so shine before men, that they may see your good works and give glory to your Father who is in heaven." (Mt 5:16)

How then can our life become a living bond uniting the Eucharist with the world in which we live and work? How can we take into the world the joy which the disciples experienced when they met their Risen Lord? This is the question to which the third part of this pastoral letter, the part on prayer, will try to give an answer.

MAN, THE IMAGE OF GOD

God is hidden, but He reveals Himself in the love He has for each one of us. It is God's love which makes it possible for us to approach Him and to be in communion with Him — in spite of our sinfulness.

"What is man that Thou art mindful of him?" (Ps 8:4) According to the Bible man was created in the image and likeness of God. The divine image in him was tarnished by sin. However, in Christ, the New Adam, the image of God is restored to its original beauty and brightness.

As members of the Holy Church, the Body of Christ, men also have been called to participate in Christ's glory, to "escape from the corruption that is in the world because of passion, and become partakers of the divine nature." (2 Pet 1:4)

Thus, escape from the corruption caused by passion is possible only in communion with God. This communion is established in Holy Baptism. There man is born anew of water and the Spirit, and God begins to work in him. God offers His help but it is up to man to long for and seek purity of mind and heart. This, again, is realized in that purposeful inner striving, that ascetic struggle which has been called "unseen warfare."

OUR INMOST SELF

In nature there is an unavoidable opposition between light and darkness: when the light grows stronger darkness is driven away and vice versa. The same kind of natural order prevails in man, in his spiritual life. The Apostle calls this opposition an internal war: "For I delight in the law of God, in my inmost self, but I see in my members another law at war with the law of my mind." (Rom 7:22)

What is the nature of this "inmost self" of ours, where good and evil, spiritual light and darkness are fighting with each other? To put it simply, we can say that we are aware of our inmost self mainly as thoughts and feelings.

When we are awake we usually do not stop thinking even for a moment. Thoughts are part of our inmost self; through them we live and act. Yet it is our common experience that we cannot always control our thoughts and feelings. We notice this, for instance, in sleepless nights when our thoughts keep running in the same circle against our will, especially when they are connected with emotional excitement.

Passions breed in the confusion of our mixed thoughts and feelings. Christ says: "From within, out of the heart of man, come evil thoughts, fornication, theft, murder, adultery, coveting, wickedness, deceit, licentiousness, envy, slander, pride, foolishness." (Mk 7:22)

Passions arise from three sources. First of all they are aroused by the outer world with its human relationships. A second source of passions is man's own corrupted nature, that "other law in my members at war with the law of my mind." It creates the lusts of the flesh, gluttony, drinking, laziness, etc. The third producer of passions is the soul's enemy, the tempter, the "spiritual hosts of wickedness in the heavenly places." (Eph 6:12) That is where unbelief, despondency, pride, and especially blasphemy, come from.

Evil has its own order of development in the inner man. The Apostle describes it in these words: "Each person is tempted when he is lured and enticed by his own desire. Then desire when it has conceived gives birth to sin; and sin when it is full-grown brings forth death." (Jas 1:15)

Can we shut our consciousness to evil thoughts so that they cannot develop into passions and begin to "lure and entice" us?

It is just as impossible for a man to prevent thoughts as it is to stop the wind by spreading one's cloak. That is what an elder told his disciple. Nevertheless there is something essential that can be done. The elder explained it in the following parable: "You are walking along a road and come to a place where there is a restaurant. Enticing odors of food come from the restaurant. But still it rests with you whether you go in and have a meal or pass by." By enticing odors the elder meant involuntary bad thoughts that enter our consciousness. We can stop to examine them: then we "go in"; in other words, we take a liking to them and admit them into our hearts. Thus we have already sinned in our thoughts and hearts. But we can also "pass by," in which case the evil thought or image that passed our consciousness is not considered a sin.

During the Vigil for the three Sundays before Great Lent, Psalm 137 is sung. It begins with the words "By the waters of Babylon, there we sat down and wept, when we remembered Zion." The last verse of the Psalm, which is usually not sung, reads as follows: "Happy shall he be who takes your little ones and dashes them against the rock!" The little ones of Babylon symbolize just those involuntary sinful thoughts and images which come to our minds as described above. They must be destroyed the moment they are born, and dashed against the rock. And this rock is Jesus Christ.

LORD, HAVE MERCY

When we stand in church we see in the icons the faces of holy people transfigured by the Holy Spirit. In the Eucharist we hear all the saints commemorated "who through the ages have been well-pleasing to God" and who are united by the Sacrament of Redemption. Like the Apostle we can say: "Therefore, since we are surrounded by so great a cloud of witnesses, let us also lay aside every weight and sin which clings so closely, and let us run with perseverance the race that is set before us, looking to Jesus the pioneer and perfecter of our faith." (Heb 12:1-2)

The glory suggested by the haloes of the saints was granted to them only when their lives of ascetic struggle were drawing to a close, and even then it happened in a visible manner only to a few. They had to start where we too must start, namely with repentance and "laying aside every weight."

The fact that in Holy Baptism we promised to renounce the tempter and stand on Christ's side is a decisive beginning. In the sacrament of repentance or confession we have renewed our loyalty to Christ and even shown it visibly by kissing the Cross and the Book of the Gospel, the Word of Christ. Yet we feel again and again that "sin clings so closely." Even the Apostle sighs: "For I do not do the good I want, but the evil I do not want is what I do," and he confesses: "I can will what is right, but I cannot do it." (Rom 7:18-19)

We all know the things that go on in our inmost selves, how evil gets a foothold and develops in our minds and hearts. We also feel our powerlessness. We are like a person besieged on all sides by a pack of wolves. What does such a person do? He climbs up the tree that is behind him and is saved. That saving tree is prayer; so the Fathers teach.

But what is prayer? According to the usual definition prayer is lifting up one's mind and heart to God. But it has also been said that prayer is the science of sciences and the art of arts. So it is a most simple thing and at the same time very rich in expressions.

Prayer gives expression to our striving towards communion with God. This communion is the natural manifestation of our love for God and of God's love for us. Through the channel of prayer we "pour out our hearts before God," which is a Biblical expression meaning that in prayer we express to God our thoughts and feelings of praise, gratitude, and worship.

However, prayer is not only a form of worship; it is also a means available to us for overcoming the evil that lodges in our inmost self. In this sense prayer is like a special line that carries man's cry for help to God.

Lord, have mercy! This is the cry for help that is repeated again and again in the service. It is also the individual's cry for help as he keeps watch at the door of his heart and cries out to the Lord to drive away the passions that creep in. This corporate and private cry for help arises from our sense of powerlessness: "Apart from me you can do nothing," the Lord says. (Jn 15:5) But it is equally strongly based on our trust that the Lord wants to purify our hearts, if only we ask. We are branches of Christ the Vine, and each branch that strives to bear fruit the Lord "prunes, that it may bear more fruit." (Jn 15:2)

Thus God's help and our own prayers will save us from "the corruption that is in the world because of passion."

TOWARD THE GOAL

"Watch at all times, praying." (Lk 21:36) What do these words of the Lord mean? Do they mean that we should constantly be ready to ward off all the evil which tries to defile our hearts? This is exactly what they do mean — we should be permanently established in such a frame of mind that we can cry from the heart "Lord, have mercy" the moment we notice evil stealing into our consciousness. Two questions confront us, however: are we able to do it and are we willing to do it?

The first question has already been answered: without help we cannot do it. As to the second question: sin has often become like second nature to us so that we do not want to lose the sweetness of the sinful thoughts and feelings in our heart and stop pampering them. But the Apostle Paul writes in his Epistle to the Philippians: "For God is at work in you, both to will and to work for his good pleasure." (2:13)

How does God work so that even the direction of our will changes? He does it by awakening our conscience and by purifying our souls. This happens, as we have said, when as members of the Church we "become partakers of the divine nature" of Christ — especially in Holy Communion. This working of the Spirit of God to purify our soul and strengthen our will is described as follows in a prayer read after Holy Communion:

Freely Thou has given me Thy Body for my food, O Thou who art a fire consuming the unworthy. Consume me not, O my Creator, but instead enter my members, my veins, my heart. Consume the thorns of my transgressions. Cleanse my soul and sanctify my reasonings . . .

Show me to be a temple of Thy One Spirit, and not the

home of many sins. May every evil thing, every carnal passion, flee from me as from a fire as I become Thy tabernacle through Communion . . .

This purification of our souls is a decisive factor, and it comes from God as a gift. What we do not get as a gift is the readiness to pray at all times, for of this it is only said that "every one who asks receives, and he who seeks finds, and to him who knocks it will be opened." (Mt 7:8) We have come back to the point where we started, to the Lord's exhortation: "Watch at all times, praying."

Prayer requires purposeful effort to the very end, and we have real reason for speaking of it as a struggle. This struggle is a necessary part of the Christian's pilgrimage through life. The word "to walk," which is often used in the Bible, aptly describes the nature of a Christian's spiritual life. It is not just being, but is always a striving forward. This is beautifully expressed by the Apostle, who says: "but one thing I do, forgetting what lies behind and straining forward to what lies ahead, I press on toward the goal for the prize of the upward call of God in Christ Jesus." (Phil 3:13-14)

We are not alone in our struggle in prayer. Countless numbers of Christians have already walked the same path as the Apostle. The Church has preserved their experiences and offers them for our use. We can set out with confidence.

THE RULE OF PRAYER

Different as we are, there is still a certain conformity in the development of our spiritual lives. So the experiences of others can serve as guides even in the life of prayer. This may be illustrated by a parable. We read an account of a journey to some distant land and we feel as if we were there ourselves. Later when we really get an opportunity to visit the same places, we recall the details we have read about and we can recognize them. This happens also with regard to prayer and to the phenomena of the spiritual life in general. We read what others have experienced and when we follow their advice we may have the same experience.

It is amazing that the spiritual directions given by the Fathers of the Church are consistent with one another regardless of when and where the Fathers lived. This is splendidly documented in the *Philokalia*, a basic work on the life of prayer and spiritual struggle. It is a large anthology containing teachings of the Fathers from the fourth century to the fourteenth, a thousand years. The conformity in the spirit of their teaching has been compared with the open sea where a large number of vessels are sailing in the same direction, propelled by the same wind. The same Spirit of God guided the teaching of the Fathers, which is based not on theory but on experience. Furthermore, man's basic nature and his basic problems have remained the same through the ages.

Regularity is the prime condition for learning to pray, according to the experience of praying people and the guidance of the Church. A specific time of the day should be set aside for prayer. By doing so we train ourselves in spiritual discipline as well. We must force ourselves to pray — so praying is a struggle to the end of our lives. The

Psalmist says: "Seven times a day I praise Thee." (Ps 119:164) Perhaps we do not set aside seven moments in the day for prayer, but mornings and evenings are natural times to pray.

What words do we use when we pray? Every member of the Church should have a copy of the Church's prayer book. It contains morning prayers, evening prayers, and prayers in preparation for Communion and for other needs. All the prayers in the Orthodox prayer book were written by the Holy Fathers. Therefore they are a school of prayer for us. They teach us to approach God in the right spirit, humbly and with pure heart, like the Fathers did when they prayed.

Besides using the prayers in the prayer book we can of course always pray in our own words as well. The time of prayer should also include a reading of suitable length from the Bible.

In order to learn to pray we should have our own rule of prayer. This means that we set regular times each morning and evening for prayer and we read a certain set of prayers at those times. As soon as we wake up we offer to God the few minutes it takes to say the morning prayers. Likewise in the evening before going to bed we read the prayers in the prayer book. This, then, is our rule of prayer. Regularity is more important than numbers of prayers. It is true that sometimes our heart may be like a fireplace that has not been heated for a long time, in which a lot of wood must be burned before it warms up.

In addition to the Scriptures a chapter from a book on the spiritual life written by an Orthodox Father should be included in our daily spiritual nourishment.

AT THE ICON CORNER

The great seventh-century ascetic Isaac the Syrian describes the essence of prayer in the following way: "The ladder that leads to the Kingdom of Heaven is hidden within you, in your own soul. Cleanse yourself from sin and you will discover the rungs by which to ascend and enter the Kingdom of Heaven."

Although the encounter with God takes place in our souls, as Isaac the Syrian says, it is important to remember that we are by no means spirits but walk in our bodies in this material world. Therefore prayer has to do with man's whole being, including his body and the environment in which he lives.

We worship God in church in a certain way, in forms created by the Holy Spirit through the centuries. Our prayer at home also presupposes a certain outward form.

When we move into a new house or apartment, the home is blessed in a religious service. The icons in all the rooms are permanent tokens of this consecration. They are reminders that God is with man in his everyday life. Every icon tells us that God came close to man in Christ in order to remain with him. "And lo, I am with you always, to the close of the age." (Mt 28:20) These were Christ's last words when He parted from His disciples and returned to heaven.

When we pray in church we have God's people -- the members of the congregation or other worshippers — visibly around us. When we pray at home we have Christ's instruction: "When you pray, go into your room." (Mt 6:6) But even so we are not alone. The icon in the corner of the room where we pray is a window into the Kingdom of God and a bond with its members.

Usually in the most central position is the icon of the Mother of God with the Son of God born Man in her arms, for this icon above all bears witness to the closeness of God. It gives us confirmation of the fundamental fact relating to our salvation: God became Man. On both sides of this central icon there may be other icons, depicting our friends in heaven whose spiritual struggle is over. Among these there is often the icon of the holy person whose name the worshipper received at baptism as well as icons of other saints who have become particularly close to him. He knows the stories of their lives and has experienced the power of their intercessions.

Before we start reading the prayers in the prayer book we ask these friends in heaven to join us in our prayer by saying the initial blessing: "Lord Jesus Christ, Son of God, through the prayers of Thy most pure Mother and of all the saints, have mercy on us." Thus we begin our prayers with the awareness of our own unworthiness and the weakness of our prayer.

Another form of the initial and final blessing which is used is: "Through the prayers of our Holy Fathers, Lord Jesus Christ our God, have mercy upon us." The Holy Fathers appealed to here are the spiritual fathers: bishops, priests, elders and each Christian's own confessor. Spiritual fatherhood is a tradition going ·back to the early Church. The Apostle himself writes: "For though you have countless guides in Christ, you do not have many fathers. For I became your father in Christ Jesus through the gospel." (1 Cor 4:15)

Fatherhood is by nature a man's role, and in the same way spiritual fatherhood, priesthood, has always been a service belonging to a man. In it he continues Christ's high-priestly service, and Christ acts through him in the Holy Eucharist. Correspondingly, the role of the Virgin Mary as the Mother of God has been raised to a more glorious position than that of the Cherubim and Seraphim. In praising the Mother of God as blessed, in accordance with her own prediction (Lk 1:48), the Church at the same time praises the work of all mothers. The biological and spiritual tasks given to mankind correspond and are complementary to one another.

But let us return to the icon corner. There it is like being in church. We light the lamp or a candle. We read prayers from the prayer book, following our own rule of prayer. We have already mentioned that each room in the house should have an icon, and this of course includes the children's rooms. Even an infant should be brought to the icon to see the flame burning in front of it. The very early years are immensely important for a child's spiritual development.

Within the home it would be a very good practice for the whole family to gather in a suitable room in front of the icon to start the day and to end it. Thus the family too would have its own short common rule of prayer, which each could then continue in his own room. In their common prayer the different members of the family could take turns reading the prayers.

The Apostle writes: "So whether you eat or drink, or whatever you do, do all to the glory of God." (1 Cor 10:31) This is why we say grace, blessing the food and giving thanks, which in turn brings God's presence into the Orthodox home.

SENSING GOD'S PRESENCE

What happens when we start reading prayers before our icon? We may soon find ourselves only reading the words while our thoughts go their own way. This may also have happened to us while we were standing in church listening to the prayers being read or sung. There our wandering thoughts did not interfere with the course of the service, but it is a different matter when we are praying alone. Prayer is prayer only when our thoughts stay with it. What should we do? We should go back to the point in the prayer where our thoughts went astray. When they scatter again after a moment, we must go back, time and time again. Also we should slow down our reading and try to pay attention to every word.

However, we may have another kind of experience. We may feel our hearts being warmed by the words of the prayer. Then the thoughts stay with it more easily. Perhaps we have experienced this in church, with the result that we did not find the service too long.

As a result of the Fall, the Fathers explain, our human nature, our thoughts and feelings as well as our bodies, are easily scattered. But in prayer, through God's grace, our nature becomes whole again. The Apostle refers to this when he says: "The Spirit himself intercedes for us with sighs when he says: "The Spirit himself intercedes for us with sighs too deep for words." (Rom 8:26) This experience, if it comes to us, is a special gift from God. Very few people are granted to keep this gift very long. It is taken away, but through it we are permitted to "taste and see how good the Lord is," so that we may know what we should strive towards or what right prayer is.

This raises the question of the role of feelings in prayer.

Should we try to pray in such a way that our feelings accompany it? The only suitable feeling is that of contrition and of our unworthiness. "The sacrifice acceptable to God is a broken spirit; a broken and contrite heart, O God, thou wilt not despise," says Psalm 51. It is in the spirit of this psalm that we should prepare ourselves for prayer, thinking of our unworthiness, but also remembering God's love towards sinners. When we stand at our icon corner in this spirit, we begin to sense God's presence in our hearts. This sense should be our constant companion.

THE RIGHT SPIRIT AND THE SPIRIT
OF DELUSION

It is a great gift of grace if a sense of God's presence awakens in us when we are praying or reading the Bible. This sense, also called remembrance of God, should be retained afterwards. As long as it prevails we can readily distinguish right from wrong and are able to experience the truth of the Psalmist's words: "Because he (God) is at my right hand, I shall not be moved." (Ps 16:8) One might even say that in this we experience what the Apostle reminds us when he asks: "Do you not know ... that God's Spirit dwells in you?" (1 Cor 3:16)

But the more precious God's gift is present in us the nearer is our spiritual enemy, trying to delude us. When a certain brother, referring to the above psalm, eagerly told his elder that he always saw God at his right hand, the elder said: "It would be better for you always to see your own sins in front of you." Thus we are warned of the spirit of delusion which is always lying in wait for one who prays. The sense of God's presence is right only when it arises within one's sense of unworthiness and sinfulness. It is like a light morning mist rising from earth that is wet with dew — from a heart softened by tears of repentance.

"I tell you this, brethren: flesh and blood cannot inherit the kingdom of God." (1 Cor 15:50) Any sensual excitement or ecstacy is a delusion of the tempter posing as an angel of light, even if miracles happen and signs are seen as well. These words of the Lord are important: "On that day many will say to me, 'Lord, Lord, did we not prophesy in your name, and cast out demons in your name, and do many mighty works in your name?' And then will I declare to them, 'I never knew you; depart from me, you evil-doers!' " (Mt 7:22-23)

When God appeared of old to Elijah on Mount Horeb, He was not in the strong wind, nor in the earthquake, nor in the fire, but in a still small voice. (1 Kings 19:11-12) The working of God's Spirit is like the still small voice in the heart of one who prays. "Learn from me; for I am gentle and lowly in heart," Christ advises. (Mt 11:29)

In prayer we encounter Christ when we pray in His name. We spoke earlier of how we must immediately try to destroy with prayer all evil thoughts and fantasies which attempt to enter our consciousness — we must dash them against the Rock which is Christ. Related to this teaching is the tradition of the prayer called the Jesus Prayer, a treasure of early Christianity which has been preserved by the Orthodox Church and which in recent years has drawn the attention of the whole of Christendom.

THAT OUR JOY MAY BE FULL

During the persecutions of the Christians Bishop
Ignatius of Antioch was sentenced to be thrown to the wild
beasts. On his way to Rome he wrote seven epistles to
different congregations. In these he mentions as his other
name Theophorus, which means either God-bearer or God-
borne. There is a tradition that he was the child whom Jesus
took in His arms when He was speaking to His disciples about who was the greatest.

When Ignatius had been brought to Rome and the moment was approaching when he was to be taken to be torn
by the wild beasts, the soldiers asked him why he kept repeating the word Jesus unceasingly. He answered that it
was written in his heart. The story is told that when the
beasts had torn him to pieces and one of the soldiers
cleaved his heart open with his sword, there really was the
word Jesus written in gold letters.

It makes no difference whether we regard this story as
a miracle or a pious legend. In any case both this and the
name Theophorus given to Ignatius show how ancient is
the practice of praying in Jesus' Name. Jesus exhorted us
in His farewell speech to pray in His Name and this was
heeded from the very beginning.

In the New Testament we see that from the beginning
the Name of Jesus contained special power. Thus when
Peter had healed a lame man and was asked: "By what
power or by what name did you do this?" he answered:
"Be it known to you all that it was by the Name of Jesus
Christ of Nazareth." (cf. Acts 4:7-10)

Jesus Himself laid stress on praying in His Name when
He comforted His disciples, who would remain in this
world:

Whatever you ask in my Name, I will do it, that the Father may be glorified in the Son; if you ask anything in my Name, I will do it. Truly, truly, I say to you, if you ask anything of the Father, he will give it to you in my Name. Hitherto you have asked nothing in my Name; ask, and you will receive, that your joy may be full. (Jn 14:13-14; 16:23-24)

Praying in the Name of Jesus Christ has been a source of joy to all generations, even to this day. This tradition of prayer has been kept especially among the hermits and in the monasteries since the fourth century, but praying in the Name of Jesus is just as much the privilege of every Christian. So it is well for us to use this tradition of prayer called the practice of the Jesus Prayer, that our "joy may be full," too.

THE JESUS PRAYER

The words of the Jesus Prayer are: Lord Jesus Christ, Son of God, have mercy on me, a sinner. A shorter form is also used: Jesus, Son of God, have mercy on me.

The Martyr Bishop Ignatius repeated the name of Jesus unceasingly. In the same way the Jesus Prayer is meant to be uttered continuously. It thus fulfills the Apostle's direct exhortation: "Pray constantly." (1 Thess 5:17)

How then does the Jesus Prayer become an unceasing prayer? We start by repeating the words continuously: Lord Jesus Christ, Son of God, have mercy on me, a sinner. We can repeat them aloud, almost voicelessly, or only silently in our minds. However, we shall learn from experience that unceasing prayer is not so simple. It has to be practiced with deliberate effort. We can set aside specific times in the day for saying the Jesus Prayer. It is also good to include the Jesus Prayer in our own rule of prayer. For instance, when we read our morning prayers we can recite it, say, ten times before each prayer. We can also sometimes start the Jesus Prayer right after the opening prayers, instead of reading the morning prayers, and then continue it for five or ten minutes, for as long as our time of prayer usually lasts. In our evening prayers we can practise the Jesus Prayer in the same way.

However, the Jesus Prayer is exceptional in that it is not meant to be said only at fixed times. The Orthodox Prayer Book says: "At work and at rest, at home and on journeys, alone or among other people, always and everywhere repeat in your mind and heart the sweet name of the Lord Jesus Christ, saying: Lord Jesus Christ, Son of God, have mercy on me, a sinner."

Is this possible? Can anyone devote himself to prayer to such a degree that he can really follow this advice?

The best answer to this question can be found by reading the book *The Way of a Pilgrim*, which has been published in a number of different languages. We shall return to the use of the Jesus Prayer in the next chapter; here we shall examine the prayer itself more closely.

If we include the Jesus Prayer in our rule of prayer, we will notice, even after practising it a short time, that it is easier for us to keep hold of our thoughts when we say this prayer than when we read other ones. This is the special advantage of the Jesus Prayer and other short prayers of the same nature; they are more conducive to concentration than those which contain many thoughts. Practising the Jesus Prayer between other prayers also helps us to read those with greater concentration.

The Jesus Prayer is said to be a perfect prayer because it contains the same basic saving truths as the sign of the Cross, namely our faith in the Incarnation and in the Holy Trinity. When we say the words "Lord Jesus Christ, Son of God" we acknowledge that our Saviour is both man and God. The name Jesus was given to Him as a human being by His mother, while the words "Lord" and "Son of God" point directly to Jesus as God. The other basic truth of our Christian faith, the Holy Trinity, is included in our prayer as well. When we address Jesus as the Son of God, not only is God the Father included, but the Holy Spirit too, for the Apostle Paul says: "no one can say 'Jesus is Lord' except by the Holy Spirit." (1 Cor 12:3)

Another reason why we say that the Jesus Prayer is perfect is because it contains the two aspects of Christian prayer. When we say "Lord Jesus Christ, Son of God," we reach up towards God's glory, holiness and love, and then with the sense of our sinfulness we humble ourselves in repentance: have mercy on me, a sinner. The contrast between us and God finds expression in the words "have mercy." In addition to penitence these words also express the consolation we receive from God's acceptance of us. The Jesus Prayer seems to breathe the Apostle's confidence: "Who is to condemn? Is it Jesus Christ, who died, yes, who was raised from the dead, who is at the right hand of God, who indeed intercedes for us?" (Rom 8:34) The heart of the Jesus Prayer, the name of Jesus, is the saving word: "You shall call His name Jesus, for he will save his people from their sins." (Mt 1:21)

THE PRACTICE OF PRAYER

It is understandable that brothers and sisters living in monasteries and convents can practise unceasing prayer — they have an opportunity to do this and they have rosaries for this purpose. But how can an ordinary Christian who goes to work and lives among people practise unceasing prayer?

This question naturally comes to mind, especially if one is already familiar with literature dealing with the unceasing prayer of the heart, such as *The Way of a Pilgrim*,[1] *Christ Is in Our Midst*,[2] *The Art of Prayer*,[3] and *St. Seraphim of Sarov*.[4] The following considerations may be of use to anyone who is seriously asking this question.

Is it really true that we have no time or opportunity to practise the Jesus Prayer?

How many things there are that we habitually do as soon as the day begins: washing, dressing, having breakfast, and so on. That is a time when our thoughts are free to repeat the words of the prayer. It is really important that as soon as we wake up we should concentrate and tune our minds to remembrance of God's presence and start to recite in our minds: Lord Jesus Christ, have mercy on me, a sinner.

Even a person who lives in the midst of a family has a chance to pray in his mind if only he remembers to do it and limits his conversation to what is necessary and useful to himself and others.

---

[1] Trans. R. M. French (Seabury Press, 1965).

[2] (St. Vladimir's Seminary Press, 1980).

[3] Igumen Chariton of Valamo, trans. E. Kadloubovsky and E. M. Palmer (Faber and Faber, 1966).

[4] By Valentine Zander (St. Vladimir's Seminary Press, 1975).

As far as the morning paper, the morning concert, and the morning news on the radio are concerned, it is for each person to consider his choice between these and prayer. Even a good thing has to be sacrificed sometimes in order to get something better in its place.

Our journey to work may take a long time. What is to keep us from concentrating on the words of the prayer while we are on the way?

Nowadays our work may be purely mechanical, perhaps just a repetition of the same movements. Here is our chance. Our hands will do their work and our minds — our thoughts and hearts — will work in the companionship of Jesus Christ. Then that monotonous work may even become pleasant, like an assignment from God. And because the practice of the Jesus Prayer improves the ability to concentrate, we need not fear that our mechanical work will be done without concentration.

However, it may be that our work is anything but mechanical. It may really demand all our thought and attention. How can we pray in that case? Certainly then it is not possible to concentrate long on reciting the name of God. Still we can do it from time to time. If we get into the habit of reciting the name of Jesus Christ in this way even for half a minute at a time — and it is possible to arrange such a pause for oneself in almost any work — remembrance of God's presence will remain as an undercurrent in our soul.

In peaceful work this is possible, but what if there is a countless number of miscellaneous things, all to be remembered and attended to? Responsibility, great numbers of duties and cares weigh heavily on our minds — but where do they actually come from? Do they not come at least partly from the fact that all those worries and duties seem to bombard us simultaneously so that we are unable to control our thoughts, but instead are controlled by them? However, if we practise prayer regularly, especially the

Jesus Prayer, we will learn to concentrate and to control our minds. The same duties and worries will still exist, but now we will know how to take up one at a time and so will be saved from the mental affliction which is nowadays called stress and which is caused by our being weighed down by everything at once.

It is doubly important for someone who has suffered from stress for a long time to change his basic attitude towards this life. It is good to remember these words of the Gospel: "For what will it profit a man, if he gains the whole world and forfeits his life?" (Mt 16:26)

Pensioners make up a considerable part of our nation today. Free from work and often living alone, their situation is ideal for the cultivation of prayer. Becoming at home with the unceasing prayer of the heart would bring real consolation to many and would provide a meaningful task: to pray for others also.

POINTS TO REMEMBER

In the preceding chapter, the book entitled *The Way of a Pilgrim* was recommended because it shows in a simple way how to practise unceasing prayer of the heart. However, it must be pointed out that the examples given in the book are exceptional cases which we cannot always apply to ourselves. In order that the reader may avoid going astray in a mysticism of the imagination or in a mere technique of meditation when he practises the prayer, we list here a number of points for the Christian to keep in mind concerning prayer.

— When you pray you meet the holy God in person.

— In order to succeed in your life of prayer, try sincerely to make your conscience clear in relation to God, your neighbour and earthly possessions.

— Nevertheless, do not hesitate to approach God in prayer, however bad you may feel yourself to be; all our sins are but a drop compared to the ocean of God's love.

— Begin your prayers humbly every day as if you were doing it for the first time; prayer does not accumulate interest, the Fathers say.

— Tune your mind to the sense of the presence of God and say the prayer unhurriedly, paying attention to every word; otherwise your prayer will be flung to the winds. When you notice that your thoughts have gone astray, simply bring them back to the words of the prayer without being disconcerted.

— Repeat the Jesus Prayer in its longer or shorter form, whichever way feels better at the time: Lord Jesus Christ, Son of God, have mercy on me, a sinner! or, Lord Jesus Christ, our God, have mercy on us! or, Jesus, Son of God, have mercy on me!

— When you are alone, sometimes recite the prayer aloud, and sometimes silently in your mind.

— When you are praying do not form any mental image of God, heaven or anything else; imagination, according to the Fathers, is a coarse mental faculty which is not suited to prayer.

— Pay no attention to impure or blasphemous thoughts or images that may appear while you are praying; they are not your own but come from the evil spirit and will disappear if you take no notice of them.

— Do not try to find the place of your heart by any special methods; this is suitable only for those who live in the stillness of complete solitude; fix your attention on the words of the prayer, and your heart will come along in its own time.

— We must force ourselves to pray throughout our lives; it is just this struggle to which Christ refers when He says that the kingdom of heaven has suffered violence, and men of violence take it by force. (Mt 11:12)

— The only feeling for which one should consciously strive in prayer is that of contrition and unworthiness; other feelings are gifts of God's grace which He grants to us according to the measure of our humility.

— Beware of taking credit for the fruits of prayer, such as concentration, emotion, tears. Often God in His mercy permits us at first to taste the sweetness of prayer, but then leaves us on our own in order to test our faithfulness and to show us what we are without the help of His grace.

— You can also recite the Jesus Prayer in church during a service and then all that you hear and see is like oil for the flame of your inner prayer. During the Eucharist, however, it is better to concentrate on the words of common prayer. According to the Fathers, the most important communion with God is Holy Communion, and the Jesus Prayer comes next.

— Every day read a chapter of the Bible and one from

the writings of the Fathers concerning prayer. Such reading is important in a time when living models and guides are lacking.

— Adopt a suitable rule of prayer and stick to it like a close friend; yet do not allow it to enslave you.

— Lastly, the most important thing to remember: Keep your heart free from hatred, envy and condemning thoughts, so that God may hear your prayer. Forgive everyone so that God may forgive you, and be merciful to all, so that God may have mercy on you. It is with good reason that the Fathers say: Your neighbour is your salvation.

CONCLUSION

This book appears at a time when there is much talk about the so-called charismatic movement. The name of the movement comes from the fact that it aims at the special gifts of grace, *charismata*, such as prophesying and speaking in tongues, which appeared in Apostolic times.

People ask whether a corresponding movement can appear in the Orthodox Church as well. The answer to this question will be a summary of all that has been said above about the Orthodox Church.

We remember that historically the one and only fountainhead of the Orthodox Church is the outpouring of the Holy Spirit at Pentecost on the fiftieth day after Christ's Resurrection. The second-century saint, Bishop Irenaeus of Lyons, writes: "Where the Church is, there is the Spirit of God, and where the Spirit of God is, there is the Church and all grace." The nature of the Church has not changed since that time. The Church is still the Church of the Holy Spirit according to Christ's promise: "And I will pray the Father, and He will give you another Counsellor, to be with you for ever." (Jn 14:16) Thus the Church as such is already a *charisma*, the gift of grace of the Spirit of God among men.

The Church is the Church of the Holy Spirit, but what about the members of the Church?

In speaking of the Eucharist we stressed the common participation of all members of the Church in the celebration of the Liturgy. We considered the matter from the point of view of common worship, since the very name liturgy means a public service. But the same matter can also be approached from the point of view of each individual faithful. The Church members do not participate in the celebration of the Liturgy only in order to make the Liturgy public worship, but also because they have all received the gift of grace, the *charisma*, for this liturgical service. When they were born again in Holy Baptism through water and the Spirit, they were at the same time appointed as a "royal priesthood" for liturgical duty.

The early Church writer Hippolytus of Rome tells how the bishop laid his hands on the newly baptized and prayed that the grace of the Holy Spirit would prepare them for liturgical service:

O Lord God, who hast made them worthy of the remission of sins through the Holy Spirit's washing unto rebirth, send into them Thy grace so that they may serve Thee according to Thy will: for to Thee belongs glory, to the Father and to the Son and to the Holy Spirit in Thy Holy Church, both now and ever and unto ages of ages. Amen.

The Apostle too is referring to this receiving of the Spirit when he says: "For by one Spirit we were all baptized into one body — Jews or Greeks, slaves or free — and all were made to drink of one Spirit." (1 Cor 12:13)

The laying-on of hands was part of the ritual of baptism in the Apostolic Age, but it can be assumed that chrismation, which soon became a permanently established custom, was also already known at that time. "But it is God who establishes us with you in Christ, and has commissioned us; he has put his seal upon us and given us his Spirit in our heart as a guarantee." (2 Cor 1:21-22) The words from the sacrament of chrismation are consistent with the above Biblical quotation: "The seal of the gift of the Holy Spirit. Amen!"

The ceremony for joining the Church through baptism includes details which are the same as in the conferring of clerical orders: tonsuring, laying on of hands, dressing in white, and the procession around the baptismal font or the Holy Table. This indicates that baptism too was recognized as an appointment to liturgical service, to the duty of the people of God as a royal priesthood. When a person is baptized or chrismated during the Liturgy, he also participates in the celebration of the Holy Eucharist for the first time.

The participation of all the faithful in Eucharistic worship is just as necessary at the participation of the priest who serves the Liturgy.

Belonging to the Church means membership in the people of God, and it means the *charisma* of the royal priesthood. However, this *charisma* does not mean separate priestly service by an individual, but always participation in the public service of the people of God in the church.

Thus every member of the Church has received the *charisma* of general priesthood and is a charismatic in the broad sense of the word. This does not mean that in addition to the general *charisma* belonging to all the Church members there cannot also be special *charismata* in the Church, granted to certain persons only, for the service of the Church.

In our discussion of the Eucharist it was pointed out that as adult baptism became less frequent, the understanding that baptism is rebirth by water and the Spirit receded into the background. In this respect there is indeed a need for improvement which could be called a charismatic revival, because its aim would be to become conscious of the *charisma* of baptism and the Holy Spirit. There are two things which must be realized in order to achieve that aim: more conscious participation in the Eucharist, and a deepening of our personal life of prayer. The Eucharist and the Jesus Prayer complete and support one another.

Can special *charismata*, such as prophesying, speaking in tongues and healing the sick, appear in the Orthodox Church? In answer we can say first of all that throughout the history of the Church, those people who have had special gifts of grace, many of whom are numbered among the saints, have not sought these gifts themselves but have come to spiritual maturity through deepest humility. Secondly, we may ask whether the Church of our day needs the same gifts of grace that were present during the Apostolic Age. According to predictions by the Fathers, there will be no signs at all in the last days, but the temptations will be so great that anyone who then perseveres in the faith will have greater glory in the Kingdom of Heaven than those who work signs and miracles.

What has been said about becoming aware of the grace of baptism is difficult enough for the Christian of today. St. Gregory of Sinai teaches:

Become what you already are,
Find Him Who is already yours,
Listen to Him Who never ceases speaking to you,
Own Him Who already owns you.